Ceolta Seisiúin na hÉireann
Irish Session Tunes

The Green Book

100 Irish Dance Tunes and Airs
Selected by Geraldine Cotter

OSSIAN

Published by
Ossian Publications
14-15 Berners Street, London W1T 3LJ, UK.

Exclusive Distributors:
Music Sales Limited
Distribution Centre, Newmarket Road,
Bury St Edmunds, Suffolk IP33 3YB, UK.

Music Sales Corporation
257 Park Avenue South, New York, NY10010
United States Of America.

Music Sales Pty Limited
20 Resolution Drive,
Caringbah, NSW 2229, Australia.

The contents of this book have been previously published
as part of Geraldine Cotter's
Traditional Irish Tin Whistle Tutor (Ossian OMB 31)

Design by John Loesberg

Special thanks to Brian Denington of *Cuirluin Prints*,
for his permission to reproduce some of his
paintings of Irish musicians.
On the cover, left to right: Conor Keane,
Francie McPeake, 'Doolin Fiddler' & Micho Russell.

Printed in the EU.

www.musicsales.com

Foreword

This book contains 100 tunes collected by Geraldine Cotter. She is from Ennis, Co. Clare, an area well known for it's rich musical tradition. Her music has been learned first hand from well respected musicians of an older generation. She is carrying on this tradition in the time honoured way, by presenting the tunes as she learnt them.

The music is written in a simple form, without ornamentation, thus making it accessible to musicians of all levels; from the beginner, to the musician who wants to increase his/her repertoire.

The tunes in this collection include jigs, reels, hornpipes, set dances, slow airs and miscellaneous pieces. The range of the tunes makes them particularly suitable for instruments that don't go below D, i.e. the tin whistle/flute/pipes; but they are equally suitable for any other instrument.

Index

JIGS

1. The Returned Yank

2. Banish Misfortune

3. Tom Friels

4. Harry's Loch

5. Donnybrook Fair

6. Gillan's Apples

7. The Hairpin Bend

8. Dan the Cobbler

9. The Burnt Old Man

10. Down the Back Lane

11. The Mug of Brown Ale

12. Molloy's Favourite

13. The Monaghan Jig

14. Tobin's

15. Do you want any more?

16. The Idle Road

17. The Shores of Lough Gowna

18. Ryan's Favourite

19. Langstrom's Pony

20. The Boys of the Town

21. Austin Barrett's

22. The Old Grey Goose

23. Petticoat Loose

24. The Pipe in the Hob

SLIP JIGS

25. Hunting the Hare

26. Open the Door

27. I have a Wife of my own

28. The Humours of Kilkenny

29. Dever the Dancer

30. Drops of Spring Water

31. An Phis Fliuch

32. Will you come down to Limerick?

REELS

33. The Sunny Banks

34. The Drunken Landlady

35. London Lasses

36. Tommy McMahon's

37. Down the Broom

38. Miss Monaghan

39. Lucky in Love

40. In the Tap Room

41. The Peeler's Jacket

42. The Flowers of Limerick

43. The Burren

44. The Golden Keyboard

45. The Galway Rambler

46. The Kerry Reel

47. King of the Clans

48. The Shepherd's Daughter

49. The Dairymaid

50. The Old Bush

51. Ah, Surely

52. Over the Moor to Maggie

53. Lucy Campbell

54. The Bank of Ireland

55. The Jolly Banger

56. The Controversial Reel

Composed by Billy McComiskey

57. The Dublin Lads

58. The Holy Land

59. Bell Harbour

60. Blackberry Blossom

HORNPIPES

61. The Rover through the Bog

62. The Kingstown

63. The Wicklow Hornpipe

64. The Clareman's

65. The Wren's

66. Dunphy's

67. Gan Ainm/No Name

68. Gan Ainm/NoName

69. The Plains of Boyle

70. Chief O'Neill's

71. The Fairies' Hornpipe

72. The Stack of Wheat

73. Off to California

74. Willy Walsh's Hornpipe

43

SET DANCES

75. The Orange Rogue

SET DANCES

76. The Blackbird

45

77. Bonaparte's Retreat

78. The Job of Journeywork

79. The Garden of Daisies

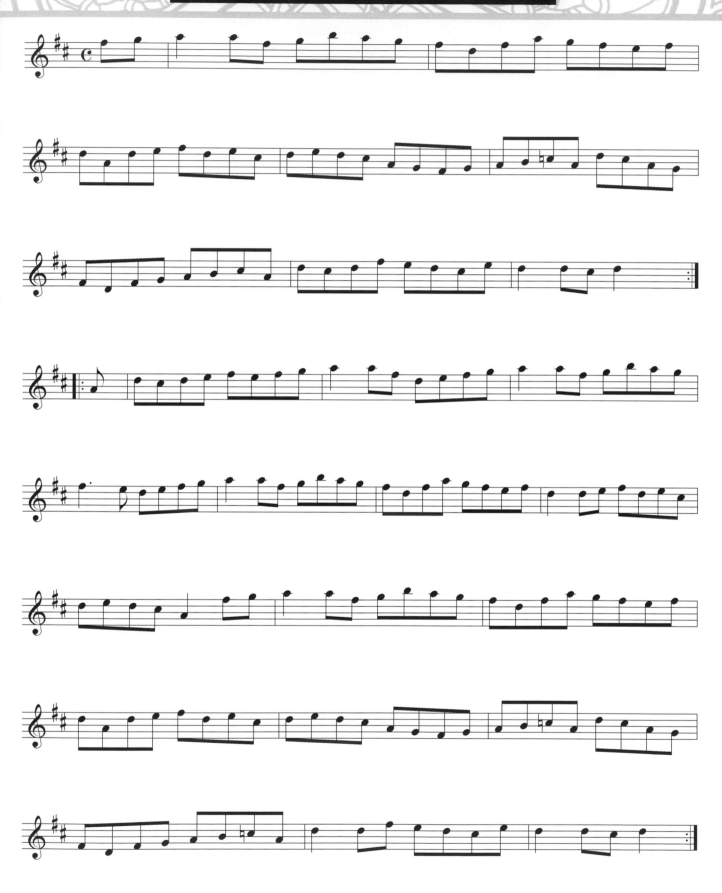

80. The Ace and Deuce of Pipering

81. The Drunken Gauger

82. The Rambling Rake

83. An Súiscín Bán

84. The Lodge Road

SLOW AIRS

85. Anach Cuain

86. Bruach na Carraige Baine

87. Cath Chéim an Fhia

88. Urchnoc Chéin mhic Cáinte

89. An Goirtín Eorna

90. An Mhaighdean Mhara

91. Coinleach Glas an Fhomhair

92. An Buachaill Caol Dubh

93. Fath mo Bhuartha

94. Cailín na Gruaige Doinne

95. Amhrán a Leabhair

QUADRILLES

96. The Cumann na mBan are Dead and Gone

97. She hasn't the Knack

POLKAS

98. Ballyvourney

99. Johnny Micky's

PLANXTY

100. O'Carolan's Draught

Ossian Publications produce a large range of Irish and
Scottish music for traditional & classical instruments as
well as collections of tunes, songs,
instruction books and items on the history of Irish Music.